Truth Be Told

By Minister Antoine R. Watson

ANTOINE WATSON

Truth Be Told

First published by Antoine Watson 2026

First edition

ISBN: 979-8-9954129-0-8

This book was professionally typeset on Reedsy.
Find out more at reedsy.com

This book is dedicated to all of God's people. whether you been saved for years, a new believer, or maybe you still live your life in complete darkness this book for you as well. May these words draw you closer to Jesus Christ, strengthen your faith, and remind you that His love, mercy, and grace are always available to transform your life completely.

Contents

Preface

This book was written from a place of transformation .

There was a time in my life when i didn't fully understand what it meant to be born again. i may have known about God, but I didn't truly know him. I didn't yet understand the depth of his love, His forgiveness, or the kind of relationship He (GOD) desired to have with me.

But everything begin to change when I encountered Jesus Christ in a real way.

Being born again is not just a phrase it points to new life. It is a complete shift in heart, mind, and direction. It is learning to love what is right, even when its hard, and turning away from the sinful desires that once felt natural. It is choosing faith when doubt tries to creep in, and perseverance when the journey becomes difficult.

This book is about that journey.

Its about learning to walk with Jesus daily, not perfectly, but faithfully. Its about understanding forgiveness not just receiving it, but giving it. Its about developing a real intimacy with God, Where prayer becomes more than words, and his presence becomes more than an idea.

Its also about the struggle the tension between the flesh and the spirit and the decision to no longer chase the things that pull us away from God, but instead pursue a deeper love in Jesus Christ.

This book is for anyone who desires more.

More than religion.
More than surface level faith.
More than temporary change.

Its for those who want a real relationship with God.

My prayer is that this book will help revive, restore, and ignite God's spirit in you to create the ability to walk in closer fellowship with your lord and savior Jesus Christ. Walk in purpose and the plan that was written over your life.

Acknowledgments

I want to give thanks to the Heavenly Father and my Lord and savior Jesus Christ for presenting me with a vision and knowledge to produce a self-publishing book to develop and change the hearts and mind of others. I am overwhelmed with joy and happiness that the lord has worked through me and for me. psalms 100 says we should enter God's gates with praise and thanks giving on our hearts.

I would like to thank my wife Keyuana Watson for helping along this journey for putting in your work on getting this book where it needs to be thanks again keep up the great work.

Thank God for all my sons they inspire me to continue on this journey as a man of God ultimately to make each one of them the best I can make them through the spirit of Jesus Christ. Antoine Watson Jr, Alexander Watson, Ashton Watson. keep this book and message in your heart always God bless you three guys you keep me going.

And last but never least all of my readers I thank God for you as well that you took time to support me on this journey God bless you all.

And I want to thank all family and friends who inspire me with your love and support. God bless you all.

1

Love

Galatians 5:22-23
But the fruit of the spirit is love, joy peace, patience, kindness, goodness, faithfulness, gentleness, and self -control. Against such things there is no law to walk in the spirit means that the Holy Spirit lives in you.

How can we remove love of the world and replace with God's love, we can't if from the time we were born until your age today living completely in darkness with the one track mind systems. The one track mind that tells us this world will be your last stop or that your mind just never think of the place that was prepared for us. Do we realize man born of this world must leave one day to be with the father, your creator, or do we feel more comfortable with this world falling into a spiritual darkness because we rather worship and idolize what the creator (God) himself has created but we don't worship the creator . (Romans 1:25) until we open up our hearts to allow God in we can never reach the loving standards of our Lord and savior Jesus Christ. I was a man on fire in the wrong way once before, attitude , defensiveness, anger, you said anything I didn't like I would match the energy instead, held on to the grudges, if they will be there I wouldn't come, and when they see me they better not say anything to me, I'm mad at them I'm sick of them, I can't stand them, they this they are that, how many of us had or still have this one track mind system. Glorify God's name if he delivered you from such ways how can we say we Love God and respect his words if we can't love one another the same love God showed us in the sacrifice of his son Jesus Christ he gave to the world. (1 John 3:11) how can we love God, by simply allowing the Holy Spirit to lead and to guide you. How do we expect to take a Godly attitude around with us if we are always thinking of this world. How many of us may encounter worldly people each day, we have to work with these type of people on our jobs also we live with them, shop with them, it can become dramatically draining to be compromised from people with spiritual blindness worldly behavior. We need to learn the difference in sinners and unbelievers, (we are all sinners bottom line) Romans 3:9-20) when you get comfortable with sin is when you become a slave to sin because you allow it to consume you in where you fall in danger zone with God and as far as being around people that don't know or Love God more than likely they won't display a Godly type of love to you because of their lack of salvation and disbelief and complete compassion for ignorance remove your self from the foolishness they will not teach you how to sustain a Godly love, Jesus hung out with sinners who believes in him, they had a chance to connect with the Lord only because their ears heard him and their hearts received him. The sinners who believes in him, they had a chance to connect with the Lord only because their ears heard him and their hearts received him the sinners he encountered most of the time faith was so beautiful in the Lord. On the other hand notice Jesus Christ never hung out with unbelievers Jesus taught us that we should remove ourselves away from the ones that do not believe in him.

2

We Found A Love

2 Corinthians 6:17-18
Therefore come out from among unbelievers, and separate yourselves from them, says the Lord. Don't touch their filthy things, and I will welcome you. And I will be your Father, and you will be my sons and daughters, says the Lord Almighty.)

It is vital we don't willingly stay in unhealthy, unhappy, anti God, worldly drooling relationships. However if you are married and your spouse is anti God or might even be a worldly type of thinker, here is the thing with us married ones, God expects us to live a Holy scripture filled life before them, we knew these things about our spouse before we married, as good as a divorce might sound because it seems like you just can't get through to your spouse, they just will not ever walk with Christ it seems like, but remember they person you fell in love with you are genuinely happy, butterflies, you probably couldn't eat, couldn't sleep you were so in love, date nights, movie nights at home, on the phone caking all day, driving pass each other homes just to feel connected. But one day after 10 kids later and bills through the roof you have disconnected from the vine it seems all most impossible to display a Godly love but God expects us to reconcile that spouse back to the father through Jesus Christ and through faith. Gold does not grant divorce because we are no longer in love, or one have God and one don't. The only way to break a covenant between marriage and God is adultery, so when God say remove yourself out from the unbelievers he means anyone outside your divined union of the marriage. (Matthew 5:31-32) in order to maintain a Godly love we must remove ourselves from the ungodly thinkers. Think about it like this one blind person is not able to see another blind person.

WORLDLY LOVE
Is based on three way artificial love.
What you can do for me.
What you can't do.
What you have done.

We Found A Love

Isaiah knew the love God was about to show the world; Our help was coming the answer to the darkness we live in was on the way. The answer to our sins was on the way. Think about the first time you fell in love with that lady of your dreams, the first time you laid eyes on her you felt like this is it, the love of my life is here, my Mrs. Good thing has arrived even felt the dark feeling of loneliness being replaced by the light of her bright smile, pretty walk, caring words, God fearing position in her heart, great cooking skills, the way she smell, her confidence, style of dress. I can only imagine the way Isaiah felt knowing we had a love on the way that would bring us light in our darkness that would sustain us through his victory he won on the cross what a beautiful love Jesus Christ shared for us all. Some one may feel like they never been loved before, all their life been looking for love and never found it. When we recognize who loved us first and turn to God and not away and know him and love God then we can fully understand how to love ourselves as well as others. Remember Jesus loves you and care for you don't waste time trying to find worldly love. Put yourself in a place in life to have an intelligent, intimacy relationship with the Lord spend time in his word each day set small goals 30 minutes per day for study time. We need to use the light that was provided as our GPS system to get to the Kingdom of God!

It's Too Dark

Why is your life upside down? Is it because you walk in complete darkness and rejecting the light, can't love right, can't keep relationships, can't shake addictions, can't keep a job, feel like you can't make ends meet, facing eviction, can't hold anything down it seems like. Well here's something to cling to, we can't be prosperous living a dark life. We have no business complaining and calling our God out on what he is not doing in our life. Have you ever took sometime to think about it? God has provided me with a light I refuse to keep on. We sometimes get comfortable with darkness. How many of you would rather have your local electric company to stop by your house and make it completely dark, no power at all for at least a month? Let's say it was a challenge you had to enter, they say no lights for a full month , no TV at all, no internet, Wow! I can only imagine that we would be so anxious, anxiety, mental breakdowns, can't see how to even cook or put your clothes on and dark restrooms. This is how we try to operate in our spiritual life, we want to function in the dark with no mind set of the proper lighting we need to provide us with a healthy spiritual filled Godly love seeking for eternal life! Why are we ok with darkness, please TURN YOUR LIGHT ON, so you can see spiritually how to use all the parts of your body God has blessed you with! For some of us we will only keep bumping into walls of life if we continue to walk in darkness.

3

Born Again

Isaiah 9:2
The people who walk in darkness will see a great light. For those who live in a land of deep darkness a light will shine.

John 1:9-11
The one who is the true light, who gives light to everyone, was coming into the world. He came into the very world he created, but the world didn't recognize him. He came to his own people, and even they rejected him.

In order to create a Christian lifestyle we have to sustain a Godly type of love.

How?

1st Jesus tells us we must be born again.

I don't remember when I was born, no one does in fact. The only thing we all know for sure we all had 2 biological parents mother and a father. We all were born of a woman. Well, all I can remember is how this St. Louis, MO dude stayed born of a woman for 42 years of his life, he grew up in church. His grandmother was the center of the family having family bible studies, church on Sunday mornings and Sunday evening dinners. All the kids would be outside playing kickball, this dude's grandmother made Sunday mornings and evenings better than any other day of the week! I know this for a fact because that little St. Louis, MO dude was me! How many of you been around the fire like me most of your life and just did not connect with Jesus Christ the right way. It's okay as long as you are still breathing it's time. Still I walked in complete darkness for the longest not allowing the power of God to lead and guide me through the Holy Spirit. You talking about nasty attitude, no one couldn't tell me anything with out me reacting in a unhealthy and ungodly manner. It came up, it came out. I was quick to let my lips and feet fail me. I never thought about how I made God feel, because I was also this selfish person not knowing and caring for other's, most likely because I didn't care to have any kind of relationship with Jesus Christ or never experienced the rebirth of the Holy Spirit. This birth we all can remember we can't stay born of a woman. We have to be reborn again of the Holy Spirit. How? Through baptism. I remember my rebirth through the spirit and how it transformed me through my awesome baptism. I was buried with Christ and resurrected with Christ as well. What happens during baptism, when you go down in the water you are burying the old person you once were, when you rise out the water it represents the new and approved person you have became in Christ Jesus, this makes you and Jesus Christ partners now.

(John 3:3-5) Jesus replied, I tell you the truth, unless you are born again you can not see the Kingdom of God. (John 3:3) 3:5) Jesus replied again no one can enter the Kingdom of God without being born of water and the spirit. (3:6) Humans can reproduce only human life, but the Holy Spirit gives birth to spiritual life.

4

Listening

It's hard for some of us to listen the right way, because we can't get over a past life experience that captivated our mental, allowing the pain from the dark past to give you a spirit of hate and bitterness. Have you ever been around someone that was just negative all the time and angry, no listening skills and all they can talk about is their past and how they just hate this person and that person? These type of people can really be chronic complainers, love can not live in your heart full of complaints and not listening, no compassion towards people, no one should have to deal with a person with a nasty attitude. Not displaying love, with no listening skills. If we encounter a person that is this way, it will make it hard for you to ever feel like you want to interact with that individual, not caring about they their title of relationship is in your life. It's best to listen always with a spiritual ear rather than a worldly ear. When we listen with a worldly ear it makes it hard to remain in self control. Unless we are reborn again, we can never bear the fruit of love and listen with a spiritual ear the way that would be a pleasing aroma to God.

Jesus told his disciples that his time was coming when he would be betrayed, but Peter tried rebuking what the Lord was telling them. Peter rather not heard the things that would happen to Jesus. Peter spirit was rebuked from the Lord and the Lord told Peter, "he was thinking like a human and not with the spirit." What happened here? Peter did not listen to the Lord with his spiritual ear he heard what the Lord was saying from a worldly ear.

Listening

How do we listen? Of course with an ear we get that, if listening with an ear is all you listen with that may be the reason your relationships never work out. It is very important to listen more than it is to speak. How many of us would rather speak than listen? We fall short of proper communication when we have the upfront attitude of always wanting to be heard, and can't be told anything. Most fights start in the home between a husband and wife because while maybe the husband speaks his concerns the wife is already thinking of a come back instead of receiving what her husband is saying or maybe the husband can't accept his wife's concerns. Listening from a macho man stand point already shutting down the feelings and concerns of his wife, or maybe its just family members you feel like you can't talk to because they have a bad time with listening. One thing all us parents know is kids that don't listen at all most of the time. My 15 year old son still don't listen; In fact my 7 year old or my 6 year old don't listen with the 2 ears our good father blessed them with. At times I wish they all had an extra ear. A piece to hear me repeating myself time after time to do your chores and for the small ones stop jumping off the ceilings. I know I'm not the only dad out here with that story. My goal is to get my sons to have the best listening skills today for the relationships they will encounter in this world and to serve others with Godly listening.

James 1:26

Understand this, my dear brothers and sisters: you must all be quick to listen, slow to speak, and slow to get angry.

Learning to listen with your heart and not your ear will give you the Godly response that will not only be satisfying to your spiritual walk it will lead others to proper communication with you.

Challenge yourself for the next 30 days to be the best listener, open up your heart and listen from there rather than the ear. When you do that your response will be more clear on who you are and what you want. Listening all the time doesn't mean you will agree but listening with the spiritual heart will teach you how to respond.

5

How To Use Your Tongue

Ephesians 4:29
Don't use file or abusive language. Let everything you say be good and helpful, so that your words will be an encouragement to those who hear them.

Be fruitful in your listening allowing the power of the Holy Spirit to lead and guide your thoughts so you can be an instrument of holiness, wisdom comes from God and it is so wise to be a great leader with great listening skills. This should be the most top priority in every ones life. How can we listen to God if we don't listen to others. Remember it is us God uses to speak through and when we don't take heed to the messenger we are not listening to the words of God. How can we listen to the words of god when some of us talk too much! Let's learn to be quiet and hear and put our mouth up for awhile.

Proverbs 21:23
Watch your tongue and keep your mouth shut, and you will stay out of trouble.

I had to learn to just shut my mouth sometimes. I remember when I had a reaction for every action. If someone said something to me that made me mad, I took quick defense to the foolishness, using my tongue, cutting that person into little pieces of ground beef leaving none left on the cutting board! COME ON NOW! You know that foul language that will make someone feel less than a human, am I the only one that has used foul language, okay maybe I am. I was a MESS before! Not using my heart to listen to all the foolishness of those who have sinned against me with foul language and thoughts using their tongue and lips for a complete tear down system. A lot of us want to use the tongue God blessed us with to tear people down. We should use our tongue to lift each other up in Christ Jesus. If we don't listen the right way with our heart then our tongue will not be used properly. Learn from me, I had to figure out how to stop letting people's bad tongues, be the reason my tongue got loose and turned into a sword, cutting and tearing people down. What am I saying, your thoughts roll off your tongue, and your tongue can send you to a burning hell if we don't learn to control it. Your tongue and how you use it is a major part of your talk with Christ. Sometimes you should listen to be quiet in the book of Isaiah he told the people of Judah inside quietness and confidence is your strength. **(See Isaiah 30:15)** Jesus Christ taught us we will be held accountable for every idle word we speak on judgment day,

(See Matthew 12:36-37). Don't allow anyone to take you there, to the point you respond with a sharp tongue. Start listening with your spirit more so you can be led to speak a godly response or the spirit may lead you not to speak at all on certain foolishness from people who are sinning against you with their words. Take a deep breathe and keep listening and the Holy Spirit will lead you through that awkward ungodly moment of communication.

6

Sinful Desires

It was awhile in life I would wake up in darkness starring at the face of sin ready to walk and talk with sin. We became close allowing me to move in the darkening of deception led and hosted by the enemy. I never realized how much darkness I was walking in, every moment of my life felt like it was okay. I thought I had the best life while being controlled completely from sin. It's like sin was okay in my life. I was cool with wild parties, drinking, smoking weed with sinners, fornicating, chasing money. It seemed like everything that was not good for me made me feel good about myself. I was taught how to be a worldly man. That's someone who was only taught that money and having women, nice clothes and going to work and back home knocking off a 12 pack of beers with a blunt rolled up with my feet kicked up on the table waiting for sports to come on television. This the way the world makes up the idea of a man. I was controlled by my sinful nature, not letting the Holy Spirit control my life. Maybe someone was like me before letting the awful desire of sin control your life leading you to a pit of fire ruling in your life because of power, you allowed sin to have over you. We have to take back our life through Jesus Christ and not let sin dominate us, living a Holy Spirit filled life through baptism and being born again of the Spirit.

Romans 8:9
But you are not controlled bye your sinful nature. You are controlled by the Spirit if you have the Spirit of God living in you. And remember that those who do not have the Spirit of Christ living in them do not belong to him at all.

Being reborn again is vital in our walk with Christ.

God created man to know and love him. But we decided to go our own way and we became slaves to sin. Baptism, good works, communion, prayer, studies in the bible are all valuable parts of the Christian life, but only faith in the death and resurrection of Jesus Christ can bring forgiveness of sin. A reborn spirit, and a relationship with God. We must reconcile our self back to God through Jesus Christ. We try to find hope in liquor, drugs, people, social media. The truth be told it's only through Jesus Christ you will find hope in life and peace he is the prince of peace, build your hope in the Lord all your help comes from Jesus Christ.

John 14:6
I am the way the truth and the life.

It was a time in my life where I looked for the truth in the world. I never thought about anything but partying, smoking weed and hanging out in the dark night clubs, waiting with all of us thirsty guys, looking to have some fun with some females night after night. We were inside darkness not knowing, because the lifestyle I was living was completely okay with me. My darkness was my light so I thought. I couldn't be told anything at that stage in the game. Darkness was a lot of fun to me and seeing the light was so far from my view. But we always have someone that prays for the light over us as we remain in the darkest shadows being led by the sin through the enemy. When I was in my twenties an older gentleman asked me are you walking in the newness of life? I thought to myself what is he talking about. The newness of life, I'm in my twenties, how can I have a new life I thought. Jesus Christ is the way, truth and life. Someone may have been like me and was so lost, believing darkness is the light walking along with the enemy day in and day out in the darkest shadows. Save yourselves RIGHT NOW, like I did! Receive your Lord and Savior and once we have been baptized then we can walk in the newness with Jesus Christ.

John 1:12-13 But to all how believed him and accepted him, he gave the right to become children of God. They are reborn not with the physical birth resulting from human passion or plan, but a birth that comes from God.

It's a difference between a sinner and living in sin. A sinner is one that just isn't perfect, they might wake up and set their day up to be perfect by abiding in Christ, you say to yourself, today I will not let anything bother me, I am a child of God, I will hold my head up high to the sky, that's what a sinner says to themselves each day. Then they leave home headed to work in their car singing and feeling good about the affirmation they just spoke this morning over the day then, BAM! Someone cut you off in traffic that triggered your frustration of all ungodly thoughts, or maybe you didn't handle a situation at work the right way.

A co-worker you don't care for always have you in a bad mood putting you in ungodly thoughts about them. The point is we just not perfect, the way we think at times makes us a sinner. We are all sinners, if you are apart of this world. But those who live in sin wake up, set out to walk with the enemy, committing murders, stealing, lying, sexual immorality, LBGTQ, I mean on and on, these people live in the dark being okay with death. Paul teaches us the wages of sin is death.

Homes

What in the world are we thinking to allow sin in our homes. Parents allow the kids to run the house these days, getting high with their kids, partying with their kids, letting sons become women and girls becoming men. Being captured and carried by sin, cheating husbands, and wives that are unfaithful. When we allow these things to take place in our homes and lives destruction will soon come. These days parents are afraid to stand up and make their kids conduct themselves as Christian people at an early age. The bible says we should train up a child the way they should go. (See proverbs 22:6) The bible also speaks on we should not spare the rod on our children (see proverbs 13:24) Jesus said bring the kids to him we should not hinder them. (See mark 10:13-16) If the bible says we are responsible for these things why are we not doing them. Some of us can't train up a dog right, let a long a child and a lot of parents spare the rod in order to gain a friendship with their children. Don't you know the bible says that is hating your kids and not loving them when you spare the rod and not discipline them (see proverbs 13:24 again) Now do this mean go find a rod and start beating your kids with it, NO... ABSOLUTELY NOT, unless you want child services at your door! The point is to have them worshiping God early and stay on them about living a healthy spiritual life style pleasing to the father do not hinder your kids from doing this. Providing them with a sinful lifestyle, sending them and the parents to eternal damnation. It's best to live for God in your youth. Do the NBA want old people or do the NFL want old people? NO, they want the youth, the young. What good would a old man be to the NBA or NFL? What good would we be to come to god old and washed up, he want us in our youth so we can work for him. **(See Ecclesiastes 12:1)** don't let the fun of our kids youth turn into sin **God said have fun inside your youth just don't forget the creator.**

7

Working for Jesus

Jesus looking for some hard workers that will stop rejecting the light (which is Jesus Christ) and come out of there darkness and shine bright to exalt his name.

The Americas dream we all was taught at an early age a man and a woman must work to provide around the house for the family. This is how we put food on the table and clothes on our back. Having a job and working is vital to the financial growth to one individuals life or to an entire family. Do you remember your first job? I do, I walked down to Hardee's restaurant trying to provide my own way to have fun and buy my own things that parents got tired of buying. I also remember how I felt, I thought I was a grown man feeling good about life making my own money. Wow! I thought this feel so good. We have for years made working for companies our main priority to the point marriages split because lack of income someone got laid off from work and it caused strain in the house and the relationship. While others feel like work, work, work, to the point it causes stress and anxiety in a marriage all they think about is the way we was brought up, work. The one thing about work we can all agree to the fact we all love payday. It's time that we teach ourselves how to work for Jesus, the pay is a lot better and once we do this we can bring spirituality to the table. The bread of life as well as the cut of the living water. We have to be willing to work for our Lord and savior he is waiting to hire you, working for the Lord is more important than you going to your worldly job each day putting food on your table. God gives us strength and gives us breath to get up and work to provide food and the things we need. We must take the same strength he gives and work for the creator. The rewards are greater then any reward that a worldly boss can give to any of us. God said a man and a woman must work for him to provide the spiritual food we need. I thought I was a real man when I got my first job at Hardee's; but I became more of a man when I realized the first time in life I'm working for the Lord.

Workouts

Physical training is good, but training for godliness is much better, promising benefits in this life and in the life to come Timothy 4:8

How many of us look at our physical form and say, I am tired of feeling out of shape, its time to hit the gym for some workouts. I know I did, I felt it was time to work on the physical body and get my health all together, so I can fell young and not feel like I'm in my 90s while in my 40s. You want to add more years to your life so you can be with family and take care of life as long as we can, looking good and feeling so great because of physical workouts. Once you arrive to your gym you will find all these people working out, focusing on physical fitness. Looking at all these ripped guys and women. You can look at the physical shape of some people in the gym and cal tell right away they have been working out for sometime, while you see others working towards getting ripped like others. Are we working out our spiritual life each and every day becoming a bible junky and not a gym junky. When we have turned our life over to the Lord we will be in shape spiritually allowing others to see the results of Love, Joy, Peace, Patience, Kindness, Goodness, Faithfulness, Gentleness and Self-Control. Being in shape spiritually is by far better than physical fitness. God would rather us to be physically out of shape and spiritually in shape. In this walk with Christ you will find that some people has been spiritually in shape for some time while others are trying to become more confident with working out spiritual muscles. Our focus should be tired of being spiritually out of shape. Did you know every time we read a scripture that is lifting spiritual weights and eventually your spiritual muscles will start to show results just like the believers who's been walking with Christ for awhile.

Workouts

We must have time out the day to work out the spiritual intellectual side of the human brain God gave us. We just have to tap into it. We can't see God workouts in our life if we always moving too fast. you have to make time for the father, slow down your mind and stop thinking all day about the horrible day you had at work or maybe at home things not right, or maybe you got upset with someone in public. You might be down and out because you have so many bills and not enough money. Have you ever heard the saying why you trying to figure it out, God has already worked it out. the fact of the matter is Jesus Christ always know what is best for your life and what's best for your life is the Lord. We can't become spiritually disabling to our life and to others by not working out your spirituality.

Here are some spiritual workouts I challenge you with for the next 3 months and if you do this it will become more and more easy.

1. Love
2. Joy
3. Peace
4. Patience
5. Kindness
6. Goodness
7. Faithfulness
8. Gentleness
9. Self-Control

Galatians 5:22

The fruit of the Holy Spirit is Love, Joy, Peace, Patience, Kindness, Goodness, Faithfulness, Gentleness, Self-control

We say three months in reference to the Trinity, The Father, The Son and the Holy Spirit.

All nine fruits can be challenging to bear. I believe a lot of us lack all nine fruits. Let's pray that for the next three months

God open you up to bear these fruits of the Holy Spirit.

Prayer

Say this prayer before the challenge start. Father here I am, ready to work out for you, come into my heart and fill me with your precious Holy Spirit so that I can bear the fruits of the Spirit in Jesus name Amen.

Workouts

The truth be told just like you can see the results of someone's physical fitness as they workout everyday, in the same way you will see the results of your spiritual fitness when you workout the spiritual muscles everyday your light will shine so bright you will blind others that's still only working out the physical life. Once before I couldn't understand what was expected of me from the father because I was too busy working in the world and not in the word of God's. Thank God he left the 99 and found one. Now my focus is and remains on spiritual fitness renewing my spiritual membership everyday by maintaining a close connection to the Lord Christ Jesus.

8

Intimacy

We must have an intimate relationship with the Lord, how?

Reading the word of God, studying the word, church services, going to bible study, praying 3 times a day like Daniel, time out every day to worship and give thanks. (Everyday for at least 30 minutes?

2 Timothy 2:15

Do your best to present yourself to God as one approved, a worker who has no need to be ashamed, rightly handling the word of truth.

There is not one relationship I know that will make it if there's never any quality time spent. Would a woman want a man that never spend time with her or would a man want a woman who never want to spend time together? The answer is NO, because everyone wants to be wanted, when there's no time put in a relationship between a woman and man it can become difficult to date leading the relationship to become a huge deal breaker. With no time how can you figure each other out and build a chemistry that would be satisfying to your heart? With no time spent it's impossible to get out of stranger zone with each other, it's hard to get a chance to know someone that barely spend time with you or no time at all.

Well don't you know if you are not spending time with God he don't know you at all and you don't know him. It is impossible to have a relationship with the Lord and you never spend quality time with him this can be a huge deal breaker to your eternal life simply because you don't study or read the word of God to gain healthy spiritual true relationship with him. Jesus will not beg you for time, will you beg someone for time? Of course not. You would like to be wanted whole heartily. Jesus said who are my true disciples, "the one that does his father's will." Not everyone that calls on his name will make it in the Kingdom some people will say Jesus we done all this good work and Jesus will reply, "I never knew you, get away :from me you who break God's laws." **(see Matthew 7:21-23)**. We must maintain an intimate relationship with the Lord in order to make it into the Kingdom of God's.

Luke 6:46

So why do you keep calling me, "Lord, Lord!" When you don't do what I say?

(To Hard in the heart)

Jesus and his disciples returned back to Jesus hometown Nazareth from a trip they took. Jesus started to teach the people. They were amazed asking where did he get his wisdom and power to perform miracles. You would think that would have won them over right? Wrong. He's just a carpenter the son of Mary, brother of James, Joseph, Judas and Simon and his sisters live right here among us. The bible said that they were deeply offended and refused to believe in Jesus. Because of the lack of intimacy they had in their hearts towards Jesus he did not do any miracles for them. Will your lack of intimacy and unbelief in the Lord stop you from receiving Jesus Christ favor?

Proverbs 11:27
He who earnestly seek good find favor.

Mark 6:4-6
Jesus told them, " A prophet is honored everywhere except in his own hometown and among his relatives and his own family. And because of their unbelief, he couldn't do any miracles among this except to place his hands on a few sick people and heal them. And Jesus was amazed from their unbelief.

Jesus will not perform miracles in your life when we refuse to worship him. We need to work towards God's favor and not just his promises. Steak life or lunch meat life.

It's a difference in believing and being a believer. A believer acts on what they believe in. Even unbelievers do that. They worship images of false God's. They act on what they believe in. You are no more than the desires of your heart. That's what you believe in. Once we understand who the source of our life is, then we will be able to bloom like a flower living life in a Christian way, pleasing the father in heaven and your Lord Jesus Christ living life now at its full potential.

Colossians 2:3
In him lie hidden all the treasures of wisdom and knowledge.

(Apart from Jesus we can do nothing)

We often suffer with depression, loneliness, poverty, lack of self control, domestic violence, no patience, alcohol abuse, substance abuse, sexual abuse, physical abuse, Sex trafficking, LGBTQ+, falling governments, low self esteem, spiritual blindness and living our life in complete darkness. These are all called devils foot holes, which will cause us to become slaves to sin. If we stay disconnected from Jesus.

John 15:1-6

I am the grapevine, and my father is the gardener. He cuts off every branch of mine that doesn't produce fruit, and he prunes that branches that do bear fruit so they can produce even more. You have already been pruned and purified by the message I have given you. For a branch cannot be fruitful unless you remain in me. Yes I am the vine, you are the branches. Those who remain in me, and I in them will produce much fruit. For apart from me you can do nothing. Anyone who does not remain in me is thrown away like a useless branch and withers.

James 1:22

But don't just listen to God's words. You must do what it says. Otherwise you are only fooling yourself.

9

Forgiveness

How many of us are holding on to old feelings that we have been feeling for awhile. You may think the way you feel is justified because of the level you were wronged on or you may think the way you feel is normal now because your spirit has gotten immune to this way of thinking for such a long time, it's became first nature to have this customized thinking. It can be nerve wracking to become this way and not realize it. You become bitter lying outside of this pool of hatred and anger and frustration leading down this path called unforgiving. Being able to forgive others is HUGE on this walk with Christ. So, many relationships have fallen apart because of the lack of loving and forgiveness. It's extremely exhausting to walk through life unbalanced having bitterness and hatred in our heart. We learned in the end of part 3 that apart from Jesus we can do nothing and we also seen all the different devils foot holes we fall into while disconnected from Jesus, not forgiving others come from lack of love and our lack of love comes from your lack inside of God.

Ephesians (4:31-32)

Get rid of all bitterness, rage, anger, harsh words and slander as well as all types of evil behavior. Instead be kind to each other, tender hearted, forgiving one another, just as God through Christ has forgiven you.

I remember being on the other side of this great **Ephesians (4:31-32)** passage carrying around bags that where to heavy weighing me down like an anchor that holds a ship in place. Have you ever been there? Am I the only one that suffered with dark anchors of bitterness, rage, anger, harsh words and slander, not caring about how I would handle certain situations using my mouth and not my heart. We can't elevate in God when we refuse to use our heart and instead ready to use harsh words that can slander someone's character. Tearing them down to the point they need to be rebuilt from the destruction our harsh words caused. In order to change this in quality you must be reborn) again. **(see John 3:3)** Once we have been born again with the Holy Spirit you can then change the way you think **(see Romans 2:2)** unless you are born again with the Holy Spirit you can then change the way you think **(see Romans 12:2)** unless you are born again you will continue to have all these ark heavy bags forcing you to death, not allowing you to walk in the freedom Jesus Christ died for. You cannot inherit the Kingdom of God living in complete bitterness and darkness. The wages of sin is death **(see Romans 6:23).**

Matthew 6:14-15

If you forgive those who sin against you, your heavenly father

will forgive you. But if you refuse to forgive others, your father will not forgive your sins.

My old middle school Brittney Woods it's in St. Louis, MO. I loved my school so much but I had a problem with this kid who thought he controlled everything and everyone, in fact we both played for the Brittney Woods marching band. I played snare drum, while he was apart of the drill team. This guy in drill rehearsal would show off in front of the girls. If you had a riffle to practice with and had it first, well this guy would take it from you. One day in drill rehearsal, I grabbed this riffle to practice with and sure enough here comes this kid with no self-control came to take it from me, he said, "that's my riffle" and I replied, "there are a thousand riffles in the barrow why do you want mine," before I could get it out fast enough he smacked me in the face using me to flex on to impress the girl students! The teacher that saw it sent him to the office and sent me to the nurse. This kid did not get suspended at all for his actions, so I'm thinking to myself you have to be kidding me, no suspension for him! That created bitterness, anger, frustration, rage, no forgiveness to this guy, all I can think about is the fact he has to pay for what he has done since he was such a school pet. They really seen no wrong with this dude. I remember the night before planning my fight for the next day all I kept saying was he is getting it nobody slaps me and get away with it. So here we are it's time to fight! I seen him coming down the hall dressed in his basketball uniform, he stared at me as he was walking down the hall as in, I smacked you yesterday and what you gonna do about it. So I punched him, he fell to the ground and I continued beating him up until I was pulled off of him! We will all keep feeling like we must defend ourselves with fights until we learn to release all the bitter bags in our life. Aren't you tired of fighting? Honestly, when we are allowing the enemy to keep smacking us around it creates bitterness, rage, harsh words and anger. We have to learn to fight the devil with the full Armor of God. Don't let Satan smack you and don't defend yourself **(see Ephesians 6:10-17)** stand firm on the foundation.

Forgiveness

1 John 3:11
This is the message you have heard from the beginning we should love one another.

How much love do we really have? God loved the world so he gave his only son to die for our sins to be able to walk in freedom because of the love Jesus showed us on the cross. Our sins were forgiving, God forgave us through his love not, not holding us accountable for our sins. They can be washed away through repentance. Each and everyday we live and mess up because of the glorious victory that was won on the cross inside Jesus Christ's death. As you see forgiving comes with love. Have you ever thought about it? What if God didn't love us we wouldn't be forgiven right, win would have power over us being our master not leaving us with opportunity to become alive through Jesus Christ. The grave would have victory and there would be no eternal life with no salvation. We would all be useless if God took away love and forgiveness. Do you know how useless you are to salvation if you have no love in your heart? With no love, how can you forgive in a Godly manner that will not impress God but please him? Get over yourself. The reason why it's important to our Heavenly Father that we forgive is because he forgave us through his son Jesus Christ. He feels like how dare those humans not forgive each other when I gave up my son to die for their sins to be forgiven, to be able to directly speak to me, to know and love me this what God is saying. forgiving and loving should be inside of you because it's inside of God and God should be inside of you. If you have not been reborn again it will be hard to bare this fruit of love. Some of us are still of the world and have not been baptized with the living water and Holy Spirit fire. God is love, right so if you don't have God it's impossible to have love and forgiveness.

1 John 3:16
We know what real love is because Jesus gave up his life for us. So we also ought to give up our lives for our brothers and sisters.

We have to be concerned for one another giving up our selfish ways to distribute a Godly love that's only pleasing to the father. God said reconcile ourselves quickly to one another after fights. We have to make up quickly, don't allow the devil to create a foot hole and control our love for one another.

Ephesians 5:1-2
Imitate God therefore in everything you do, because you are his dear children. Live a life filled with Love following the example of Christ. He loved us and offered himself as a sacrifice for us, a pleasing aroma to God.

God is Love

1 John 4:7-8

Let us continue to love one another, for love comes from God. Anyone who loves is a child of God and knows God. But anyone who does not love does not know God for God is love.

Drop Your Rocks

In the book of John Chapter 8 the religious law leaders and Pharisees brought to Jesus a woman that was caught in the act of committing adultery and wanted to bring her in front of the crowed and stoned her to death, but Jesus told them let the one who has never sinned throw the first stone. The bible said they dropped their stones leaving one by one until no one was left in the crowd, but Jesus and the woman and Jesus forgave her sins right there on the spot. He said to her go on and never sin again. We have to understand that we all have sinned and failed short of God's words somewhere in our lives it's important that we do not judge others. We need to drop our stones and forget about the sinful past in someone else's life, worrying bout someone else guilt and sinful nature, this will only have God checking you out even more, it would put you under the radar from the master Jesus Christ **(Matthew 7:3-4)** Jesus teaches us to take the log out of our eyes before we try and clean up the speck in our neighbors eyes.

10

Perseverance

How many of us know that our faith determines how we emerge from the trials life present to us? We must place our complete trust in our Lord and Savior. In life we lose love ones, we have to scratch to make a living to pay bills, health issues, kids acting up, marriage not the best, family not supportive, friends not being friends, mom walked out on you, no dad around and it just seem like in life we can never get ahead. Well, don't you know all of these challenges in life is to build character and position inside of you. Notice I didn't call these challenges of life issues. They are not issues we have, they are called training wheels. Look at all the challenges of life as if God is training you for something great; which would be the purpose you were created for. We allow challenges of life to become a devil's foot hole because of the way we accept life from God, most of the time our acceptance for life challenges we to afraid to face them so they turn into complete complaining and discomfort and unbelief in God. Do you know the devil is watching? How we handle the responsibilities the Lord gives us. If he see that you are disorganized spiritually he will roll on you captivating your mental telling you life is too hard to bare, because Jesus says the Devil is the father of lies. **(see John 9:45)**

Perseverance

1 Timothy 6:11
But you, Timothy, are a man of God; so run from all these evil things. Pursue righteousness and a godly life, along with faith, love, perseverance and gentleness

What is perseverance: It is not the mind set of a worldly thinking person. If you are a slave to sin, being led and controlled by the power of sin, then realize this one thing. A perseverance mind set is far from you. If you like drama and love trouble and your feet is quick to fun to evil, it sounds like the enemy has you locked up and you are drifting away from faith, love, perseverance and gentleness. Perseverance is often created inside of a person the moment they have been reborn again and accepted Jesus Christ as their Lord and Savior. The Holy Spirit is a gift and its given only to those who have been baptized and became new with Jesus. Peter explained this fact in **(Acts 2:36-41)** it's the Holy Spirit that gives you the power to persevere, we see Paul told Timothy that because you are a Godly man. You can persevere through the darkness and evilness of the world. How many of us are disconnected from Jesus and when we go through things or know someone that's going through, we use the word perseverance. For example, if you had a friend and that friend was getting beat up from life, they lost a job on top of that their house was foreclosed on, kids acting up, marriage on bad terms and no money in the bank. I mean that friend is just really going through and not only is the friend going through they are completely disconnected from Jesus Christ and now that friend is a slave to sin. Then here comes the good-hearted friend taking the life of their friend in complete consideration, by saying to the friend you have to persevere that has absolutely no relationship with Jesus Christ. In order to persevere in life we must be connected to Jesus. **(See John 15:4-5)**

Perseverance

Truth be told is that we all must hold on to God's understanding, unfailing, faithfulness, love and all his promises in order to persevere in a godly manner, that will not allow us to fall into sin as we persevere through the adversity's and pain that life can bring our way. If we take the P.E.R out of perseverance that spells SEVERANCE. When we say severance it means to end a relationship or connection with someone, so when we go through we need to make sure we persevere with God and not end our relationship or separate from God. Don't give God a severance pay check by leaving him outside your life. You are reborn again, you can now persevere like a pro in the game, taking full control on the field tackling bad health issues, in between jobs and don't know how you will make away, gas cut off, lights about to be cut off, you can barely eat sometimes, single parenting, kids are being rebellious, no support from family, God is really testing your faith, but because you are apart of God now just persevere your way through these hard times in life. When we have patience of a saint, God will show up and make every situation you had to persevere through your victory, story, for his glory.

Perseverance

We can't use God in away that will help us persevere through life, because when trouble come some people run to superficial sources, alcohol, drugs, people, internet, medium, sex, money, all type of impurities that we turn to and allow them to lead and guide us whenever we feel a storm of life coming. It's all deception from the enemy to tell you to be led by such superficial sources we only persevere through the supernatural God.

11

Faith

Every morning we get up and plan our day with coffee, breakfast, grab our phone to check notifications, check the to do list, then we warm up our cars to prepare for the ride to work to get the day going as usual not even thinking is there something off with this day. It's the same routine you repeat every single day all year. So it becomes something that just comes so easy to us not to think about. We have gotten to the point we have put faith in the routine that seems to be the core of our lives. It's no problem for us to get up in the morning and hop right in the car not even giving no thought will the car start are not, you put your complete faith in the motor just knowing it will get you around the city and back home.

Faith

Our savior should be the core of your life that you put faith in, each morning God wakes you up, not putting any thoughts in the day and what it may bring because you have allowed Jesus to be the motor that gets you to and from in spirit each day you live. Jesus to be the motor that gets you to and from in spirit each day you live. Eating the word of God each morning from breakfast and drinking the blood of Jesus down in your soul. It is impossible to please the father without faith. We need to repeat Jesus in our heart every day making him new regular routine and not a rotation meaning only serving him every once in a while. Your faith is only as strong as your relationship with Christ Jesus. Only the power of Jesus can give you the strength and confidence you need to build up your faith. The worldly things we put faith inside of has absolutely no means to keep you they are powerless, things didn't make man. God made man to make things so the power and your faith comes from the one that created all things.

God's plan from the beginning was to give us salvation through Jesus Christ (Faith) Abraham is the father of faith, because God would use him to bless every nation through the seed that would come from his line. The greatest descendant of Abraham would be Jesus Christ. Abraham was not made right with God because of his good works, it was faith that made him righteous with the God of Israel. The same today we need to put nothing but compassion and complete obedience and faith in our God. **(see Genesis 12:2-3, Genesis 15:6) (Galatians 3:6)**

Faith is sealed the moment the body dies. The soul separates from the body leaving judgment on the spirit and depending on where your faith pointed to (Christ) determines where you will spend eternity. So it's very important to know that not all of us will rest in peace. Only the spirit that died inside of faith will find rest for it. But the one that will die outside of faith will be given the spirit of torment. **(see Isaiah 57:1-2, Isaiah 63:16)**

This why we must be careful about saying we are saved by grace. We are not saved by grace, you are saved through faith in God and because of that he offers you his grace and mercy. (see Ephesians 2:8-9) often we use faith in a absolute deceiving way. For example, you have heard many times before someone say keep the faith and God will provide you with the job. I don't mean to be a bearer of bad news, but faith is only for eternal purposes not for gifts. Faith is when a sinner is made righteous with God by faith through Jesus Christ our Lord and savior. Faith is accepting Jesus as your Lord and savior and nothing else. Hope is what you put in Christ for the things we need in the everyday life food, water, shelter, good health, income etc. Let's not mix faith with hope they have to different meanings.

Hope = waits for it happen future expectations
Faith = believes it's already true, present certainty.
So (Faith) is like the foundation - it believes.
(Hope) is like the fruit it expects.

(see Hebrews 11:1) be blessed in your faith keeping your spirit inside of the Lords creating a strong bond with God, to allow strong holds to be lifted from God. Remember your FAITH determines how you emerge from trials life will present to you. You must place your complete trust and faith in our Lord and Savior the same way God showed us through the father of faith Abraham.

12

Conclusion

My Prayer for you is that Faith, Love, Intimacy, Perseverance, Forgiveness and the lack of sinful desires will follow you in Christ Jesus our Lord and Savior who reign in peace, power, love, compassion, mercy and grace to all people of all nations. Minister Antoine hopes and pray that this book will help lead and guide you to the path of truth Jesus Christ our Lord and Savior. Share this book with others you may think is ready for the truth. We all can play our part in the building of God's kingdom simply by speaking and sharing the gospel of truth Jesus Christ the Messiah the Holy one.

About the Author

Minister Antoine is the founder of Man On Fire Ministry in St. Louis, MO. Striving to bring humanity back to Christ through book writing, podcasting, encouraging encounters of the Lord and different out reaching. Man On Fire Ministry will continue to work with and for God until our mission and community services are completed unto the Lord. Our mission and goal is to shepherd the lost sheep of God's and to glorify God's throne by doing everything we do for eternal purpose and not for self nor personal gain. We are controlled and committed to the power of the Lords Holy Spirit.

You can connect with me on:

- https://www.mofm.info
- https://www.facebook.com/profile.php?id=61571201432791

Also by Antoine Watson

I'm passionate about sharing practical insights and inspiring stories that encourage growth and reflection. Through my writing, I aim to connect with readers on a personal level, offering guidance, encouragement, and a fresh perspective on life's challenges and opportunities.

Truth Be Told
Writer and speaker sharing God's truth to inspire faith, hope, and transformation in everyday life.

www.ingramcontent.com/pod-product-compliance
Lightning Source LLC
LaVergne TN
LVHW011052110826
845149LV00015B/3466

* 9 7 9 8 9 9 5 4 1 2 9 0 8 *